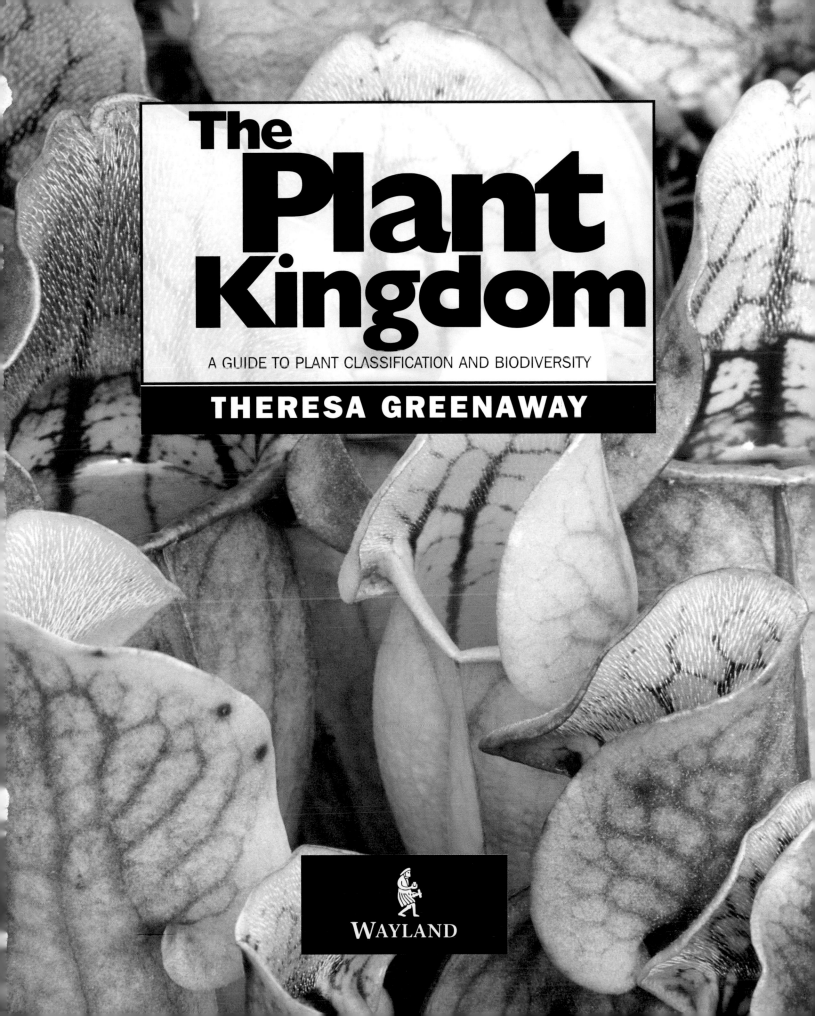

The Plant Kingdom

A GUIDE TO PLANT CLASSIFICATION AND BIODIVERSITY

THERESA GREENAWAY

WAYLAND

First published in 1999 by Wayland Publishers Limited
61 Western Road, Hove, East Sussex BN3 1JD, England

© Copyright 1999 Wayland Publishers Limited

British Library Cataloguing in Publication Data
Greenaway, Theresa
   The plant kingdom: a guide to plant
   classification and biodiversity. –
   (Classification)
   1.Plants 2.Plants – Classification 3.Botany –
   Environmental aspects
   I.Title
   580
ISBN 0 7502 2456 8

Edited by Philippa Smith and Margot Richardson
Designed by Simon Borrough
Printed and bound in Italy by G. Canale & C.S.p.A

Cover captions: main picture: *Bird of Paradise flower* (Strelitzia reginae). Small pictures, from left: *'Lobster Claw'* (Heliconia wagneriana); *Wellingtonia* (Sequoiadendron giganteum); *Korean fir* (Abies koreana); *Claret cup cactus* (Echinocereus triglochidiatus); *Lotus flower.*

Title page: *North American pitcher plants* (Sarracenia purpurea) *are carnivorous. They have water-filled leaves that trap insects.*

Below: *A tree unfurling its new leaves is a sure sign that spring has come.*

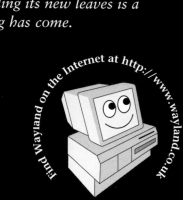

Find Wayland on the Internet at http://www.wayland.co.uk

Contents

Kingdoms of life

HUMANS ARE JUST ONE OF MILLIONS of different kinds of living organisms alive today. No one yet knows just how many different kinds, or species, there are, and more are being discovered all the time. To make the study of this enormous variety a little easier, and to ensure that one form of life is never confused with another, living organisms are sorted or 'classified' into groups according to their similarities and differences. Biologists refer to this huge wealth of species as diversity.

Classifying living things

Scientists who classify and name living organisms are called taxonomists. Scientific classification begins by sorting organisms into very large groups called kingdoms. Classification systems are constantly being reviewed, but most scientists believe that there are five of these large groups:

Animals Multicellular, mobile organisms that eat food by swallowing.

Plants Multicellular organisms almost all with leaves, stems and roots, that contain green chlorophyll for photosynthesis.

Fungi Mushrooms, toadstools, moulds and mildews that absorb food.

Protists Seaweeds and single-celled organisms that photosynthesise or eat food.

Monerans Bacteria, very simple micro-organisms that photosynthesise or absorb food.

The kingdoms of life are divided into smaller groups called phyla (singular phylum). Each phylum is divided into classes, the classes are divided into orders, and the orders are divided into families. Each family is divided into genera (singular genus), each of which may contain one or more species.

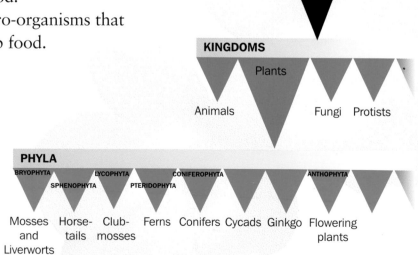

LIVING THINGS

KINGDOMS

Plants

Animals   Fungi Protists

PHYLA

BRYOPHYTA   LYCOPHYTA   CONIFEROPHYTA   ANTHOPHYTA

SPHENOPHYTA   PTERIDOPHYTA

Mosses   Horse-   Club-   Ferns Conifers Cycads Ginkgo Flowering
and   tails   mosses   plants
Liverworts

The plant kingdom

All living plants are included in one of the phyla on page 4. This book concentrates on mosses and liverworts, horsetails, ferns, conifers and flowering plants.

Naming names

Most familiar plants have common names, such as oak or poppy. But worldwide, there are about 800 species of oak, and over 120 kinds of poppy. To add to the confusion, a common name in one country may apply to a quite different kind of plant in another. For example the name toothwort means quite different plants to American and British botanists. Clearly, a universal system for classifying plants and all other living organisms is essential.

Biologists use a system of classification devised by the Swedish botanist Carolus Linnaeus (1707–1778). Every plant and other living organism is given its own unique Latin name. These Latin names may seem difficult to remember at first, but soon become familiar. Each name has two parts. The first part tells us to which genus the plant belongs. It always begins with a capital letter. The second part tells us which particular species it is.

What is a species?

The word 'species' describes a group of very similar living organisms that are able to breed with each other to produce fertile offspring. A species is the basic unit of classification. Occasionally different species of plants interbreed and may produce offspring. These are called hybrids. Although hybrids may be healthy, they are often infertile.

These foxgloves (Digitalis purpurea) *belong to the genus* Digitalis *and the species* purpurea. *The species name always begins with a small letter.*

Mosses and liverworts

MOSSES AND LIVERWORTS are grouped together in the phylum Bryophyta. They are small plants anchored by fine rhizoids instead of true roots. They may form clumps or tufts, or spread out over a surface to make a network of trailing stems. All mosses and some liverworts have thin, simple leaves. The rest of the liverworts are made up of flat, plate-like green lobes called a thallus.

The flat lobes of this liverwort branch and spread over damp, shaded rocks.

Characteristics of bryophytes

▶ Plants with two distinct stages, or generations; a green moss plant (gametophyte) and a smaller, dependant sporophyte (capsule, stalk and foot)
▶ Gametophyte lives for quite a long time, maybe several years
▶ Archegonia and antheridia well-developed
▶ Male sex cells need moisture so that they can swim to the female sex cells.

Bryophytes are divided into two main classes:

Liverworts

- may be lobed or leafy
  leaves in three rows
  leaves never have midribs
- capsules borne on weak, colourless stalks
  capsules usually round and split into four parts when ripe
  spore capsules contain spirally thickened organs, 'elaters', to help disperse spores.

Mosses

  always leafy
  leaves usually stick out around stem; do not always appear to be in rows
  leaves often have a tiny midrib
- capsules borne on thin, wiry stalks, often brightly coloured
  capsules oval or oblong, lid and peristome teeth open when ripe
- no elaters.

Gametophytes and sporophytes

The development and appearance of all living things is governed by genetic material contained in their cells. Genes are arranged along chromosomes, rather like a string of beads, and each species has a characteristic number of paired chromosomes. This is the diploid state. During sexual reproduction, genetic material from the male fuses with that of the female. To prevent doubling of chromosomes every time this happens, the sex cells contain just one of each pair of chromosomes – they are haploid. After fertilisation, each seed or spore has the correct number again. In plants, the haploid stage is called the gametophyte. The diploid stage is called the sporophyte.

Life cycle of mosses

Mosses and liverworts do not have flowers or seeds, reproducing instead by means of spores. As in all plants, the life cycle is made of two stages, but what separates bryophytes from all other groups is that it is the gametophyte that grows into the familiar green moss plant.

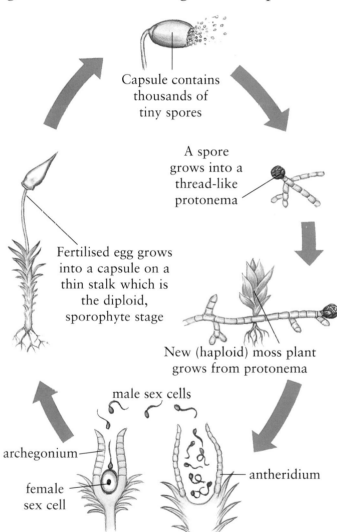

Capsule contains thousands of tiny spores

A spore grows into a thread-like protonema

Fertilised egg grows into a capsule on a thin stalk which is the diploid, sporophyte stage

New (haploid) moss plant grows from protonema

male sex cells

archegonium

antheridium

female sex cell

A moss plant produces male and female sex organs called antheridia and archegonia. Each minute male sex cell has two tiny 'tails', called flagella. When they are released from the antheridia, they are attracted to a ripe archegonium by chemicals it secretes. They swim inside to fuse with, or fertilise, the female sex cell or egg.

7

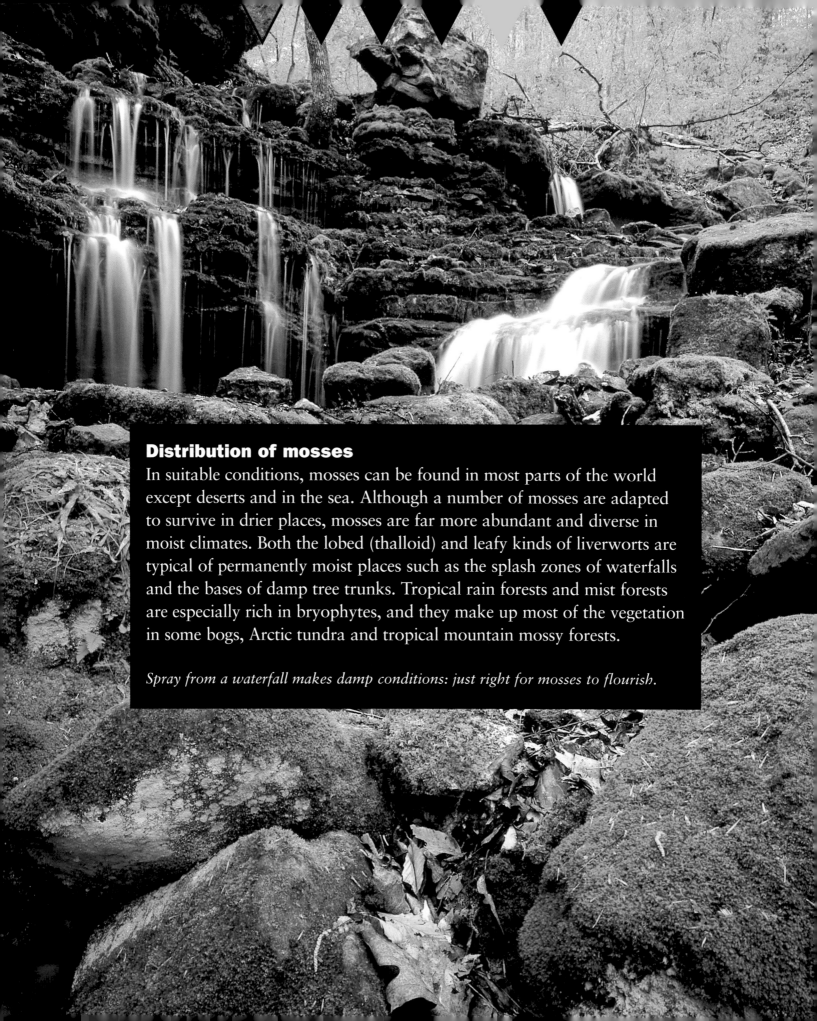

Distribution of mosses

In suitable conditions, mosses can be found in most parts of the world except deserts and in the sea. Although a number of mosses are adapted to survive in drier places, mosses are far more abundant and diverse in moist climates. Both the lobed (thalloid) and leafy kinds of liverworts are typical of permanently moist places such as the splash zones of waterfalls and the bases of damp tree trunks. Tropical rain forests and mist forests are especially rich in bryophytes, and they make up most of the vegetation in some bogs, Arctic tundra and tropical mountain mossy forests.

Spray from a waterfall makes damp conditions: just right for mosses to flourish.

▼ *The moss* Polytrichum commune, *showing moss capsules. Each capsule has a tiny lid, and sometimes a hood. When ripe, the lid falls, revealing a closed ring of teeth.*

How mosses live

Mosses make their own sugars by means of photosynthesis, but they also need water and mineral nutrients in order to grow. Most mosses simply absorb water, and minerals dissolved in it, through their leaves. But some mosses, for example *Polytrichum*, have underground stems that are able to absorb water, and simple vascular tissues to carry it up the plant. Mosses that take up water and nutrients through their leaves also absorb unwanted chemicals, so they are easily affected by environmental pollution.

Surviving drought

Mosses of dry places frequently have leaves that are drawn out into long, white hairlike tips. These reflect heat, and help to trap moisture in the moss tuft. As they dry, the moss plants shrivel, but they can quickly revive after rain.

Leafy liverworts

At first glance, a leafy liverwort looks just like a moss. But a moss has leaves that stick out all round the stems, whereas those of a liverwort are arranged in three distinct rows, two along the upper side of the stem and one row hidden from view on the underside.

On a dry day, these teeth flick open, and the spores are shaken out. They may be carried long distances on the wind.

Horsetails

TODAY THERE ARE NOT MORE THAN thirty species of horsetails in the phylum Sphenophyta. In the Carboniferous Period (about 345–280 million years ago), horsetails made up a significant part of the swampy vegetation. They were medium to tall, tree-like species. The living descendents of these long-extinct horsetails are all stiffly upright, small to medium-sized plants.

Whorls of branches circle the stems of horsetails, and the leaves are no more than small scales. This is the horsetail Equisetum telmateia.

Characteristics of sphenophytes

▶ Land plants with two distinct stages, or generations: a long-living horsetail plant (sporophyte) and a tiny, short-lived prothallus (gametophyte)

▶ A creeping, perennial underground stem (rhizome) that sends up vertical shoots

▶ Upright stems which bear whorls of green branches

▶ Vascular tissues in stems, roots and branches

▶ Leaves are brown, straw-coloured or colourless, reduced to tiny clasping scales in whorls around stems

▶ Reproduce by spores produced in a cone-like strobilus at the tip of fertile shoots

▶ Each spore has four 'arms' (elaters) that help them to disperse when they are shed.

Life cycle of horsetails

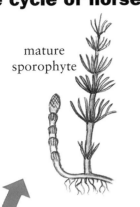

mature sporophyte

Spores develop in strobili at the tips of fertile shoots.

Each spore has four minute 'arms' (elaters) which can move with changes in humidity.

When clumps of tangled spores land on moist ground, each germinates and grows into a prothallus.

female sex cell

male sex cell

Male and female sex organs develop on the underside of the prothallus. The male sex cell swims to and fertilises the female sex cell. A fertilised egg then develops into a new young horsetail plant.

Giant horsetail

Although clearly similar to a living horsetail in appearance, the now extinct *Calamites* was 10 metres tall. It flourished in the low-lying Carboniferous swamps that covered much of the land surface. At this time, the climate was warm and humid. As the plants that made up the dense vegetation died, they fell into the stagnant swamps to make a thick peaty layer that eventually turned into hard, black coal.

Lycophytes

This separate phylum of plants contains about 1,100 species of clubmosses and spikemosses. In spite of these names, they are not related to mosses. They have a life cycle similar to that of horsetails and ferns. The clubmoss plant (sporophyte) is small to medium in size. It has creeping or trailing stems and upright shoots. All are covered with small simple leaves. Spores develop at the base of special leaves called sporophylls. When released, each spore grows into a prothallus (gametophyte). Clubmoss prothalli grow underground. They may take years to germinate, and then may not produce sex cells for another fifteen years.

Stagshorn clubmoss (Lycopodium clavatum) *growing on moorland.*

Ferns

THE FERNS, phylum Pteridophyta, are the most diverse of the spore-producing plants. They have a well-developed vascular system, and in all but a few species their fronds have a layer of waxy cuticle to prevent them drying out. They vary in size from small plants with fronds only a few centimetres long to tall tree ferns many metres in height. In common with the horsetails, the dominant stage of a fern's life cycle is the sporophyte: the leafy fern plant.

The fern plant

A typical fern plant has an underground stem, or rhizome. Roots grow from this for anchorage and to absorb water and nutrients. Leafy fronds also grow from the rhizome, either forming a rosette or an irregular clump. Fertile fronds bear spore-producing organs, in patches called sori (singular sorus), usually on the lower surface of the frond. The shape and position of the sori, together with the shape and appearance of the fronds, are characters that biologists study in order to identify different species of ferns.

Characteristics of pteridophytes

▶ Land plants with two distinct stages, or generations: a small, medium or large sporophyte, the fern; and a tiny, fragile short-lived gametophyte, the prothallus
▶ Underground stems, (rhizomes), from which leaves (fronds) arise
▶ Vascular (conducting) tissues in stems, roots and leaves
▶ Fronds tightly coiled in bud stage (with a few exceptions)
▶ Spores develop inside tiny stalked capsules called sporangia, that are usually clustered in patches called sori.

◀ *The underside of a fern leaf, showing the sori and sporangia. This type of fern,* Dryopteris, *has little papery flaps which cover the sporangia while they are developing.*

▶ *Fronds of ostrich ferns* (Matteuccia struthiopteris) *unfurling.*

Life cycle of ferns

Fern plant (sporophyte) produces fertile frond that has patches of sporangia in sori on underside of frond.

The first egg cell to be fertilised starts to grow into a tiny new fern plant.

Male sex cells swim from the antheridium to the archegonium in a film of moisture.

archegonium — male sex cell

antheridium

As the wall of each sporangium dries, it ruptures at a weak point called the stomium, flicking out the ripe spores.

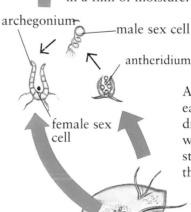

female sex cell

A spore that lands on damp soil germinates and grows into a flat, roughly heart-shaped prothallus (gametophyte) less than 1 cm long. Antheridia and archegonia develop on the lower surface.

Growth of a frond

Fern fronds take a long time to develop. Inside each bud the frond is perfectly formed, though very small and tightly rolled. When it starts to grow, the coiled, unrolling blade and lengthening stem are often called croziers or fiddleheads. Growth is rapid because all the cells of the frond simply have to expand.

Simple blade

Fern diversity

Ferns show considerable diversity, but still depend on moisture in order to reproduce. Once the fern plant is established, many kinds can withstand much drier climates than other spore-bearing plants such as horsetails and clubmosses. Ferns can therefore flourish in many parts of the world, although they are absent from the coldest and driest areas. One species can even live in salty mangrove swamps. But it is the warmer, wetter parts of the world where fern abundance and diversity are highest. There are 12,000 different species of ferns that can be arranged in about twenty families.

Tripinnate ferns have blades divided three times, giving the whole frond a lacy appearance.

Frond shapes

A fern frond has a stalk, or stipe, and a leaf blade with a midrib, or rachis. The frond varies in shape. Its blade may be simple, or divided into leaflets called pinnae. The pinnae of some species are divided again into smaller leaflets, or pinnules.

Pinnate frond

Palmate ferns have fronds divided like the fingers of a hand.

Bipinnate frond

Filmy ferns are very delicate and shrivel and die in all but the most humid conditions. Their fronds are only one cell thick. Most species live in wet, shady tropical forests, but a few species can survive in wet forests in west Britain and the Pacific forests of North America.

Water ferns (Azolla) float freely on the surface of lakes and ponds. Their roots dangle into the water. Each frond has two lobes: an upper, hairy lobe that floats, and a thin, lower lobe that stays underwater and bears the sporangia.

Tree ferns (pictured on page 44) have an upright, woody stem or trunk, at the top of which is a crown of large fronds. As an old frond dies and falls off, it leaves a scar on the trunk. Tree ferns are mostly found in the tropics and the subtropical regions of the southern hemisphere. There are about 350 different species. The black tree fern (*Cyathea medullaris*) of New Zealand is the tallest: it grows up to 20 metres in height.

Bracken is one of the most familiar ferns. It grows all round the world, and is a serious weed in many places. Bracken spreads quickly by means of deep underground rhizomes. It is an unpopular plant with farmers because the arching fronds may reach two metres in height, shading the light from valuable pasture grasses. These fronds are poisonous, so if livestock eat them they may become ill.

Plants with seeds

ALL THE PLANTS LOOKED AT SO FAR – mosses, liverworts, horsetails and ferns – reproduce by means of spores. Spore-bearing land plants evolved about 420 million years ago. The first seeds are thought to have appeared about 100 million years later, borne on plants that palaeontologists call 'seed ferns'. This group became extinct, but their descendents, cycads, conifers and flowering plants, are the kinds of plants that cover most of the Earth's surface today.

A mountainside covered in a variety of flowering plants, in Colorado, USA.

Differences between seeds and spores

Spores
▶ are very small, only one cell
▶ do not carry food reserves
▶ are carried, or spread, by means of wind or water.

Seeds
▶ are made of many cells
▶ each contains a tiny embryo plant
▶ carry food reserves, in the form of oils or starch, in seed leaves (cotyledons) or endosperm
▶ are carried, or spread, by wind, water or animals.

Seed-plant reproduction

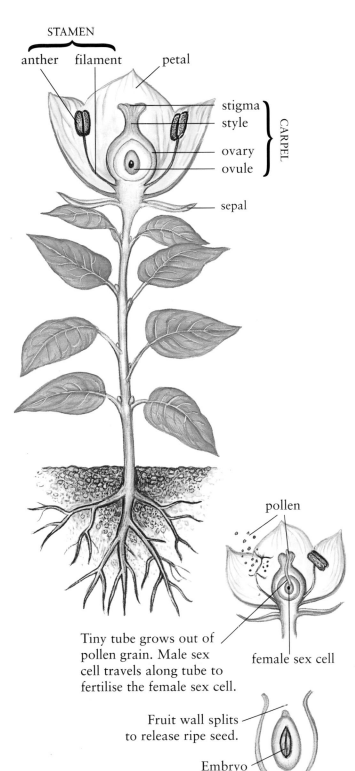

STAMEN

anther filament petal

stigma
style } CARPEL

ovary
ovule

sepal

pollen

Tiny tube grows out of
pollen grain. Male sex
cell travels along tube to
fertilise the female sex cell.

female sex cell

Fruit wall splits
to release ripe seed.

Embryo
inside seed

Fertilisation

The male sex cells of lower plants need water so that they can swim short distances to the female cells. Male sex cells in seed-producing plants no longer need to swim. They have become enclosed in the very tough outer coat of pollen grains. Wind or animals carry pollen to the female sex organs. Then a tiny tube grows out of the pollen grain, and the male sex cell travels along this tube to fertilise the female sex cell in the ovule. These evolutionary developments resulted in the tremendous diversification of seed plants.

Cycadophytes

Cycads are seed-bearing plants that grow in tropical and sub-tropical parts of the world. They resemble tree ferns or palms, although they have more similarities with living conifers and ginkgo (see page 21). Pollen grains are produced in cone-like structures, and are carried to female cones by wind or beetles. But unlike all other seed plants except ginkgo, the male sex cell inside the pollen grain still has flagella.

About 250 million years ago, cycads were a diverse and widespread group of plants. Now, only about 160 species are still living. Many of these are on the verge of extinction, caused by over-collection by plant hunters.

Dominant plants

Seed-bearing plants make up most of today's land vegetation. Except for a few highly specialised exceptions, they all have roots, stems and leaves. They have diversified and adapted to many different climates. Humans, and all other land animals, are dependent on these plants, directly or indirectly, for food and shelter.

Conifers

THE MOST FAMOUS CONIFERS are probably those used as Christmas trees, but these are just a few species out of the 520 or so different kinds that are included in the phylum Coniferophyta. Conifers are either trees or woody shrubs. The name of this phylum means 'cone-plant'.

Larches are one of the few kinds of conifer trees that shed their leaves in autumn. The slender needles turn bright yellow before falling.

Characteristics of conifers

▶ All trees or woody shrubs
▶ Mostly evergreen with a few exceptions
▶ Leaves are leathery needles, straps or ovals; some tiny and scale-like
▶ Contain sticky resins
▶ 'Naked' ovules lie on scales usually arranged in cones
▶ Seeds either develop in cones, or sit in a fleshy cup or aril
▶ The dependent gametophyte is reduced to just a few cells.

Most conifers are evergreen, which means that they are leafy all year round. When they are young, a single leading shoot and the growth of whorls of branches at fairly regular intervals gives conifer trees a typical triangular or flame-shaped outline. This may be lost as the conifer ages.

Cones

Male and female sex organs are borne in separate cones that are made up of a number of small scales attached to a central spike. Male cones are small and light. They fall after the pollen has been shed. The pollen is light and powdery and is carried on the wind. Some lands on young female cones, but most pollen is wasted. The scales of a young female cone are soft and slightly open. Pollen of the same species landing extends a pollen tube into the ovule. The scales then close. Some female cones take as long as three years to mature. By this time, the cone is much larger, and it is heavy and woody. The scales open on a warm day to release winged seeds.

Cone diversity

Cones differ in size and appearance. They may be extremely hard with thick woody scales, or have much lighter, thinner scales. Some kinds have sharp spines or bristles on each scale. A few kinds have fleshy scales, so the cone looks like a berry.

On this branch of a Korean fir (Abies koreana), *you can see unopened male cones (clusters of tiny pink cones), a young female cone (an upright, crimson cone) and a woody mature female cone.*

The Italian cypress (Cupressus sempervirens) has a very narrow crown and dark green foliage. These trees are a common sight on the dry rocky slopes bordering the Mediterranean Sea.

Conifer distribution

Conifers occur in both northern and southern hemispheres, but the species from the south are very different in appearence from their northern relatives. The largest conifer forests are the boreal forests of northern Canada, Europe and Asia. Conifers also form forests on the slopes of most of the world's mountain ranges. Their narrow leaves are tough enough to withstand very cold winters, and their downward sloping branches mean that snow can slide off causing little damage.

In the south, conifers grow with broadleaved trees to form the mixed forests of New Zealand, Australia, South Africa and South America. The climate here is damp, mild and frost-free.

Diversity

There are seven families of conifers. The pine family, pines, spruces, firs, larches and cedars, and the yew family, all have narrow leaves or 'needles'. The cypress family has tiny scale leaves. Conifers are arranged according to the differences and similarities of foliage, cones and other seed-bearing structures.

Cypresses

This genus contains about twenty species. The leaves are small and scale-like, and are arranged close together along the shoots. Monterey cypress is so tolerant of salt-laden winds that it is often planted in areas near the sea.

Fir trees

These typical conifers are tall trees with slender, spire-shaped crowns. There are about fifty species of firs. The leaves are narrow, often sharply-tipped, needles. When they are ripe, the cones disintegrate.

Silver fir grows on the mountains of Central Europe. Noble fir grows from north of Washington to central Oregon, along the Cascade Mountains, in the USA.

Yellowwood trees

Conifers belonging to this genus grow in South Africa, New Zealand, Australia and South America. Their foliage is leathery and narrow. These conifers do not have cones. The seed stalks are fleshy, swelling as the seeds ripen so that each sits in a brightly coloured cup.

Veteran trees

Many species of conifer trees live for a very long time. There are living wellingtonias and coast redwoods in North America that are over 2,000 years old. In New Zealand, kauri trees can also live for over 2,000 years. The record, however, is held by bristlecone pines in Arizona and Nevada, USA, some of which may be as much as 5,000 years old.

Ginkgophytes

The ginkgo tree is often described as a living fossil. Native to China, it is now planted in many other countries. It is the only remaining species in the phylum Ginkgophyta, which was at its most widespread and diverse in the Jurassic Period (195–141 million years ago). Like conifers, ginkgos grow into tall trees, but like cycads and lower plants, the male sex cells can move by lashing minute flagella.

The distinctive fan-shaped leaves of the ginkgo (Ginkgo biloba) *make this tree easy to identify .*

Flowering plants

FLOWERING PLANTS make up the largest phylum of living plants, the Anthophyta. (Until recently, this group was known as the Angiospermae). They may be tall trees, shrubs, or low-growing and herbaceous (non-woody). There are about 250,000 different species of flowering plants. As well as the flowers that make this group distinct from all others, the seeds of anthophytes are completely enclosed inside a structure called a fruit. Everyone knows that peaches are fruits, but so too are inedible poppy capsules, lupin pods and acorns.

Characteristics of flowering plants

▶ Can be trees, shrubs or herbaceous
▶ Mostly land plants, but a number live in water, a few even in the sea
▶ Have roots, stems, leaves, flowers and fruits
▶ Have flowers that are made up of sepal, petals, male stamens and female carpels (see page 17)
▶ Pollen grains contain the male sex cells
▶ The female sex cell, the ovule, is completely enclosed inside an ovary
▶ After fertilisation, the seeds develop inside the ovary, which is then called a fruit.

◀ *Common poppies* (Papavar rhoeas). *Annual poppies flower all at the same time. This ensures that they are cross-pollinated by bees carrying pollen from one flower to another.*

Annuals

These are plants that live only a short time. They can germinate, grow into a leafy plant, produce flowers and set seeds in just a few weeks. Some may live for a few months, but generally, by the end of the summer, annuals have shed their seeds and died.

Biennials

Biennials, such as foxgloves (pictured on page 5), germinate and make a rosette of leaves one summer, overwinter like this, and then grow a tall flower spike the following summer. By autumn, all the seeds have been shed, and the plant dies.

Perennials

Perennial plants may live for a number of years. Herbaceous perennials sprout a clump of flowering shoots every spring, then die back in autumn. Their thick roots, swollen with food reserves, lie dormant until the next spring. Shrubs and trees may lose all their leaves in autumn, but the woody stems or trunks stay alive, growing a little thicker every year. Anthophyte trees are commonly known as 'broadleaved' trees, to distinguish them from coniferous 'needle'-leaved trees. Although broadleaved trees do not reach the great ages of conifers, many species will live for 300 years or more.

The woody shrub Pacific dogwood (Cornus nuttalli) *growing among towering wellingtonia trees,* (Sequoiadendron giganteum) *in California, USA.*

Distribution

Flowering plants make up most of the vegetation of tropical jungles, the grassy plains of the steppes in Asia and the prairies in North America, the temperate woodlands, moors, swamps and marshes. Flowering plants are vitally important to people – for food and many other uses – and for their beauty, scent or spiritual importance. This has meant that humans have always carried important plants with them on their travels. Plants that are well established in other countries are called introductions.

Anthophytes are divided into two classes, the monocotyledons and the dicotyledons.

Dicotyledons

The dicotyledons make up the largest group, or class, of flowering plants. It includes all the broadleaved trees, as well as many smaller plants, arranged in 249 families. The name of this group means 'two seed leaves'. Lying between the seed leaves (cotyledons) is the tiny embryo that will start to grow into a new plant when germination begins. The seed leaves are thick because they are full of food reserves that nourish the developing embryo until it is a seedling large enough to start making its own food by photosynthesis.

Characteristics of dicotyledons

▶ Two seed leaves (cotyledons) in the seeds
▶ The primary root (first root to grow from the seedling) lengthens and branches out into secondary roots
▶ Plants may be herbaceous or woody
▶ Vascular system arranged in a ring, or cylinder, inside each stem
▶ Leaves have a network of veins; they are often broad in shape and frequently have a petiole (leaf stalk)
▶ Flower parts – petals, carpels etc. – usually in fours or fives
▶ The pollen grains generally have three furrows or pores.

Vascular system

A plant's vascular system carries food and water to all parts of its leaves, roots and reproductive organs. Water and minerals absorbed through the roots are carried to all other parts of the plant in the xylem. Dissolved sugars are carried from the leaves to the rest of the plant and down into its roots in the phloem. These tissues are arranged in strands.

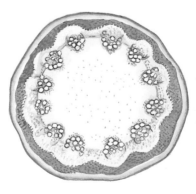

◀ *Cross-section of a typical diicotyledon stem: the vascular bundles are arranged in a cylinder inside the stem.*

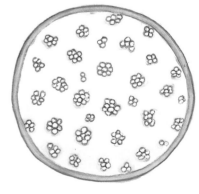

◀ *Cross-section of a typical monocotyledon stem: the numerous vascular bundles are scattered throughout the stem.*

Germinating seeds

All seeds need moisture, warmth and oxygen. Some seeds may stay dormant (inactive) for months, or even years, until conditions are right, and germination can begin. A seed that is ready to germinate absorbs moisture, and the cotyledons begin to swell. Chemical changes mean that the food stored in the cotyledons starts to pass into the tiny embryo. Each embryo has a minute shoot (plumule) and root (radicle).

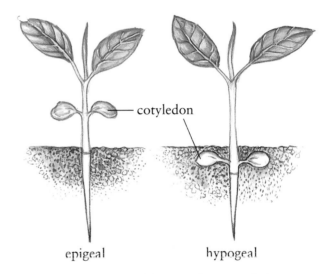

epigeal   hypogeal

Some plants have seed leaves that stay below ground: hypogeal germination. Others have cotyledons that emerge above ground and turn green: epigeal germination.

Size range

Dicotyledons have a wide size range. Some alpine saxifrages make leafy tufts no more than two centimetres in height. The Australian mountain ash, a kind of eucalyptus tree, reaches heights of 105 metres. If plants grow in poor conditions, they may never reach their full height. A hawthorn bush sprouting from a rocky outcrop will be much shorter than a nearby specimen with its roots in deep soil.

Conspicuous petals surround the reproductive parts of each of these dog rose flowers.

The dicotyledon flower

The parts of flowers are arranged in whorls, although in some kinds this arrangement is difficult to make out. Those of dicotyledonous flowers are present in fours or fives, or multiples of these numbers. The outer parts are called sepals. Their function is to protect the other floral parts when they are in bud, and in some species, to contribute to seed dispersal.

The petals may be clearly visible and scented to attract insect pollinators, but wind-pollinated flowers have insignificant petals or none at all. A whorl of stamens produce the pollen. In the centre of the flower, the female reproductive parts are arranged in carpels.

Monocotyledons

The second group of flowering plants is known as the monocotyledons, because they have one seed leaf or cotyledon. The plants in this group are mostly small to medium sized and herbaceous. It also includes palm trees, which are tall plants with woody trunks, although these do not grow in quite the same way as broadleaved trees. Grasses, orchids, lilies and daffodils, and fruits such as pineapples and bananas, are all monocotyledons.

Lily flowers show clearly that the floral parts are arranged in threes or multiples of three.

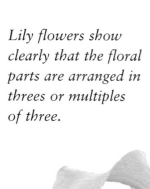

Characteristics of monocotyledons

▶ One seed leaf (cotyledon) in the seeds
▶ The primary root (first root to grow from the seedling) soon dies, then a root system of fibrous, adventitious roots develops
▶ Plants are usually herbaceous, but may be woody
▶ Vascular system scattered across stems with no definite arrangement
▶ Leaves usually have parallel veins; they are often long and narrow in shape and seldom have a stalk
▶ Flower parts are usually in threes or multiples of three
▶ The pollen grains generally have only one furrow or pore.

The monocotyledonous flower

As with dicotyledons, the monocotyledon flower is basically arranged in whorls, but the floral parts are in threes or multiples of three. In some families, the sepals and petals are indistinguishable, and are called tepals. Monocotyledonous flowers may be very attractive, such as those of orchids and lilies, or very small and insignificant, for example those of grasses and sedges.

Orchids

The orchid family contains about 18,000 species. Orchids occur everywhere except on a few remote islands and Antarctica. The flowers of orchids have distinctive characteristics. The sepals look like petals, but one of the three true petals, called a labellum or lip, is very different in shape, and often colour, from the other petals.

Palms

The palm family contains about 2,800 species. Some are low growing, clumpy plants, but most are tree-like, with a tall, unbranched trunk and a crown of huge leaves, or fronds. A palm grows taller from a single large bud in the centre of its crown. If this dies, or is cut off, the whole tree dies. Palm fronds are either shaped like a feather or like a fan. The largest leaf of all flowering plants belongs to the raffia palm (*Raphia farinifera*).

Unlike dicotyledon (broadleaved) trees, palm trees do not grow thicker every year. This is because their vascular strands are scattered across the width of the trunk, and not in a cylinder. It is the cylindrical growing layer (cambium) in conifers and broadleaved trees that produces the annual increase in thickness.

Date palms (Phoenix dactylifera) *have been cultivated for at least 3,000 years. Their edible fruits are part of the diet of many people who live in the deserts of north Africa and the Middle East.*

Flowering plant diversity

THE DIFFERENT SPECIES OF PLANTS that grow in an area, country or continent are collectively referred to as its flora. Species that occur naturally in a country are said to be native. Different parts of the world have very different floras. This has come about due to a combination of factors. The main factors are climate, and the way the tectonic plates that make up the Earth's crust have moved over the many millennia during the evolution of plants.

Holarctic

Paleotropical

Neotropical

Cape

Australian

Holantarctic

Floristic regions
Botanists divide the Earth into six floristic regions. These divisions reflect the flora in relation to climate and changes in the Earth's crust.

Worldwide families

Some families of flowering plants are found all round the world. The buttercup family has about 1,800 species, with representatives in all parts of the world except Antarctica.

The creeping buttercup (Ranunculus repens) *occurs naturally from Britain eastwards right across Europe, temperate Asia to Japan, and it has been introduced to America and New Zealand.*

Islands

Sometimes hundreds of kilometres away from the nearest continent, islands very often have distinctive floras. Species of plants may be found that occur nowhere else on Earth. A species that only grows in one particular area is said to be endemic to that area. About 95 per cent of the flora of the Hawaiian Islands is endemic. Often whole genera of plants are found nowhere else.

Australia

The continent of Australia is a vast island that separated from the land mass of what is now Antarctica many millions of years ago. Its flora is so distinctive that it forms a single floristic zone. Perhaps the best known of Australia's special plants are the gum trees: about 600 different species of *Eucalyptus*. These have diversified to survive in most Australian habitats, from the moist temperate forests of Victoria and Tasmania to the dry grassy plains of central Australia.

The flowers of the red-flowering gum (Eucalyptus ficifolia), *which grows in Australia.*

Richest of all

Rain forests have a larger diversity of plants than any other habitat, and the Amazon rain forest is richest of all. In just one hectare, two hundred different species of trees have been recorded. The whole of Europe north of the Alps and west of Russia, possesses only fifty species of native trees. In addition, rain forests contain many different species of smaller flowering plants and climbers, as well as a wealth of ferns, mosses and liverworts. It is this great diversity that makes rain forests so valuable

Grasses

Without doubt, the grass family is the most important family of monocotyledonous plants. It contains about 8,000 species. A handful of these species provides the bulk of the diet for most of the world's population. These are commonly known as grain, or cereal crops, and some of them have been in cultivation for at least 10,000 years. Without wheat, rice, maize, barley, oats, rye and millet how would we survive? Many more kinds of grasses make up the pastures upon which livestock, as well as herds of wild animals, feed.

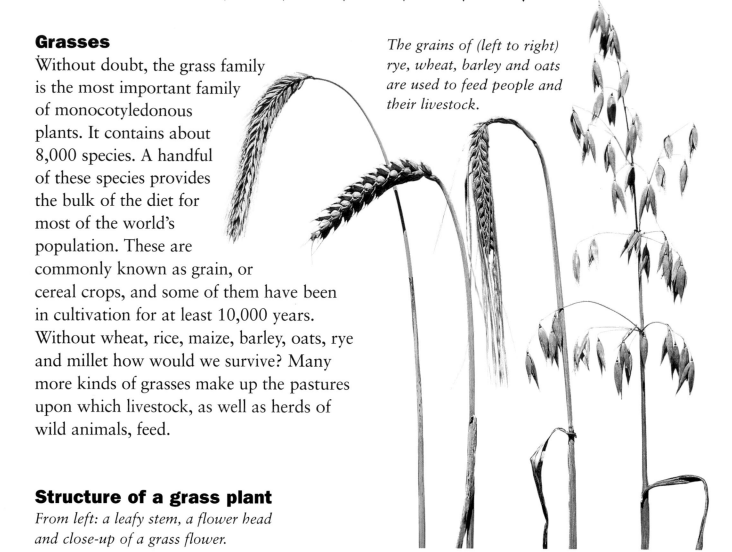

The grains of (left to right) rye, wheat, barley and oats are used to feed people and their livestock.

Structure of a grass plant

From left: a leafy stem, a flower head and close-up of a grass flower.

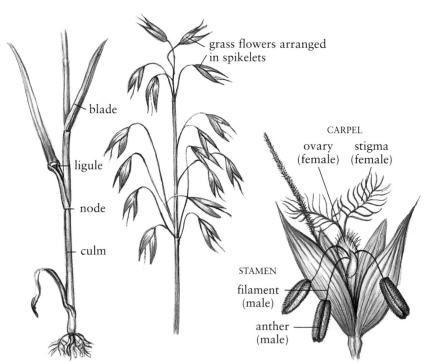

blade

ligule

node

culm

grass flowers arranged in spikelets

CARPEL
ovary (female)   stigma (female)

STAMEN
filament (male)

anther (male)

The grass plant

Grass plants can grow closely together. Each plant produces branches called tillers at ground level, so it can be impossible to tell where one plant stops and another begins. Below ground, a mass of fibrous roots binds the surface layer of the soil into a tough mat or turf.

Grasses are wind-pollinated, producing masses of dry, dusty pollen that cause hay fever in many people. The thin fruit wall remains tightly pressed to the grain, or seed, of the grass.

Why grass can be grazed

New leafy grass shoots grow from buds that are close to the ground. Grazing animals such as cattle, horses and sheep bite the shoots off just above the buds, so that they can continue to grow and produce more shoots for the grazers to eat. Only if there are too many animals on a pasture does overgrazing mean that these buds are nipped off as well. In addition, the leaves continue to grow from a basal growing point. If the upper part of the leaf blade is eaten, the rest of the leaf can continue to grow.

Bamboos

This group of grasses is rather different from the rest. Bamboos have tough, woody stems that have leafy branches near the top. Some species grow very tall and tree-like. *Dendrocalamus giganteus* has stems that reach 35 metres. There are about 830 species of bamboos, distributed in Central and South America, Africa and parts of Asia. They are most abundant beside water, on damp mountain sides and in rain forests.

Springy turf

We play golf, football and cricket on carefully tended sportsgrounds and golf courses. The species of grass chosen to plant for this purpose are selected to make a close, thick hard-wearing turf. Regular mowing keeps the turf in good condition.

Huge clumps of pampas grass (Cortaderia selloana) *grow on the plains of Argentina. The large silver-white plumes of the female flower head are familiar in many countries because this grass has become a popular garden plant.*

Useful flowering plants

It is easy to appreciate the usefulness of plants that we use directly, such as vegetables, fruit and timber, but it is not quite so easy to appreciate just how much we rely on others. Paper is made from pulped wood, from both broadleaved and conifer trees. Soap is often made from coconut or palm oil, and castor oil is used in racing-car lubricants. Cork is used for thermal and acoustic insulation. Chewing gum consists mostly of the sap of a tropical tree, and sugar comes from cane or beets.

No matter where they originally came from, most fruits and vegetables are now available all around the world.

Fruit and vegetables

Apples, bananas, mangoes, potatoes, tomatoes and cabbages are all fruits and vegetables from flowering plants. They are now grown in many parts of the world, but originally, apples and cabbages came from Europe, mangoes and bananas were from tropical Southeast Asia, and potatoes and tomatoes grew only in South America.

Grains

The wild ancestors of modern cereal crops had much smaller grains. Cultivation of wheat and barley began about 10,000 years ago, and rice and maize are thought to have been in cultivation for about 5,000 years. Rice is usually just cooked and eaten, but wheat and rye are mostly made into flour. Maize has many uses, including the production of corn oil used for cooking.

Fibres

There are about thirty species of cotton plants (*Gossypium*), native to parts of Africa, Asia, Australia and the Americas, but most of the cotton produced today comes from just one species.

Drinks

Starting the day with a cup of tea, coffee or hot chocolate is part of the way of life in many countries. Tea is made from the young shoot tips of the tea plant *Camellia sinensis*, which originated in China. Coffee, originally from the Ethiopian highlands of Africa, is prepared from the roasted seeds of some *Coffea* species. The plant that gives us cocoa and chocolate, *Theobroma cacao*, comes from the Amazon rain forest.

Medicines

Some plants produce chemicals that taste dreadful. This is to try to stop animals from eating all their leaves and flowers. Many of these chemicals are also extremely poisonous, but often yield valuable medicines. For example, poisonous foxgloves are used in the preparation of the drug digoxin, which is prescribed for certain heart conditions.

Rubber

Tyres are made from rubber prepared from the sap of a tree that is native to Brazil, but which is now also grown in plantations in Southeast Asia. Natural rubber is hard to work with, but chemicals are added to stabilise and harden it.

Cotton fibres are found in the large fruit capsule, where they are attached to the seeds. Their natural function is to help the seeds disperse when the capsule splits open.

Vital requirements

PLANTS NEED SUNSHINE so that they can make sugars by means of photosynthesis. They need water to keep their cells firm, for photosynthesis, transport of dissolved nutrients and sugars, and for all other biochemical processes. A variety of minerals is also necessary for growth. They need oxygen to breathe, and enough warmth for all these processes to work successfully. They also need to reproduce themselves and spread out, or disperse.

Welwitschia mirabilis is a slow-growing plant from the Namibian Desert. Each plant produces a single pair of very long leaves. Dew condenses on these and trickles down to its roots.

Diversity

Plants live in different habitats all round the world, from icy tundra to mild, moist forests and hot, dry deserts. As they have evolved, they have been able to colonise all but the most inhospitable areas. A vital requirement that may be in abundance in one environment may be in very short supply in another. Some plants are suited to hot, dry climates where water is scarce but there is plenty of light. Others thrive where there is plenty of moisture, but little light. Soils may be waterlogged or infertile. The adaptations that mean survival under all these conditions all contribute to the tremendous diversity of the plant kingdom.

Photosynthesis

Plants can make, or synthesise, simple sugars from water and carbon dioxide by harnessing the energy in sunlight. This process is called photosynthesis and is shown below.

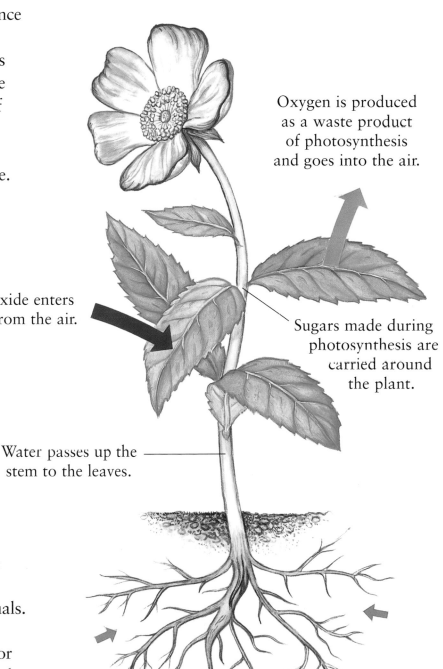

Oxygen is produced as a waste product of photosynthesis and goes into the air.

Carbon dioxide enters the leaves from the air.

Sugars made during photosynthesis are carried around the plant.

The energy in sunlight is used by the green leaves to power photosynthesis.

Water passes up the stem to the leaves.

Competition

Different species of plants seldom grow in isolation, and there may be just a few of one kind, or perhaps quite a number of different individuals. Their roots compete for water and minerals and their leaves compete for light. Obtaining enough of these vital requirements means the difference between survival or death.

Water is absorbed by the roots.

Reaching the sun

Sunlight is essential for photosynthesis. Where a lot of plants grow close together, they struggle to compete for light. Each plant needs to have as much leaf surface as possible exposed to the sun's rays. In forests, the trees themselves compete against each other for light, and the forest floor may be quite dark. Smaller forest plants are either adapted to make the best of low light levels, or they have diversified in a number of different ways to compete with the forest giants.

By the time the woodland trees have a crown of foliage, these wood anemones (Anemone nemorosa) *will have finished flowering and their leaves will have died away.*

Temperate woodlands

Broadleaved trees of Europe, Asia and North America shed their leaves during autumn. The woodland floor is therefore much lighter in winter and early spring, so many smaller plants grow and flower before the trees open their new leaves.

Tropical forests

Rain forests have a leafy canopy all year round. The forest floor is quite dark and very humid. Many tree seeds germinate, but can grow very little unless a nearby tree topples down, creating a clearing into which light floods. This is the trigger for new tree seedlings to race upwards towards the sunlight.

Smaller plants have a number of ways of obtaining enough sunlight.

Climbers use the tree trunk as a support. Species of *Philodendron* climb up a tree trunks, attaching themselves with tiny adventitious roots that sprout along the stems. Eventually they reach the canopy, and sunlight. The lower parts of the stems may then die away. Climbers are often called lianas, or vines. Rattan palms have small sharp hooks that they use to scramble to the top. Others, such as passion-flowers, have tendrils. Vines twine around each other to make a thick rope.

Epiphytes are plants that lodge on the branches or trunks of rainforest trees. They use their host as a means of getting enough light. Species of orchids, bromeliads (members of the pineapple family), mosses, liverworts and ferns have all adapted to live high up in the canopy. Here their leaves can catch the strong tropical sunshine.

The roots of epiphytic bromeliads cling to the bark of trees. Often the whole branch is covered with many kinds of epiphytes.

Down below

Some plants remain on the gloomy forest floor. Instead of trying to reach more light, these plants have accessory pigments in their leaves that help them to make the best use of the light that does reach them. These additional pigments are purply red, and this colour often masks the green colour of the chlorophyll. Arums such as *Alocasia* can grow in quite heavy shade. The leaves are silvery or coppery on top, and deep purple-black underneath.

Warmth

In the Arctic tundra, plants have a very short growing season. The liverworts that grow in some of the bleakest parts of the tundra are found in cracks in the ground. They look nearly black. The dark-coloured pigments absorb warmth, as well as helping to make the most of the light. These plants grow very slowly indeed.

Surviving drought

Plants that grow in dry areas are adapted to survive with little or no water for weeks, months, or perhaps even years. In the warmer, tropical parts of the world, the year is not divided into summer and winter, but into the wet season and the dry season. The length of the dry season varies. In the monsoon forests of tropical Asia, it lasts for several months. To conserve water, the forest trees shed their leaves. They remain leafless until the monsoon rains fall.

Deserts

Rain may not fall for years in the driest deserts. There are a number of ways that plants manage to survive. Some have very long roots to reach moisture deep below the surface of the ground. Cacti and other succulents have thick, fleshy green stems that store water.

Annual desert plants survive as buried seeds. After a good soaking at the onset of a rainy spell, these germinate and grow very quickly. As they come into bloom, the desert is a blaze of colour. They pass through their entire life cycle in a few weeks, leaving a new crop of seeds for the next rains.

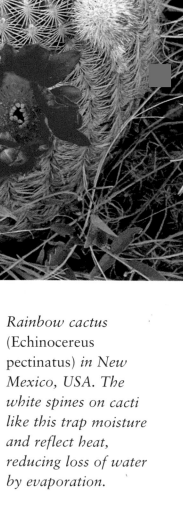

Rainbow cactus (Echinocereus pectinatus) in New Mexico, USA. The white spines on cacti like this trap moisture and reflect heat, reducing loss of water by evaporation.

It's hard at the top

Epiphytes flourishing in the rainforest canopy also suffer from drought, even though it may rain nearly every day. The rain comes down in torrents, but it runs off the branches just as quickly. There is no deep soil to hold the rain, or in which these plants can root. When the sun shines it is very hot indeed, and water soon evaporates.

Epiphytes often have thick, waxy leaves to prevent evaporation. These leaves are sometimes arranged in a rosette, so that rain runs back towards the centre of the plant and its roots. The bases of the tough leaves of tank bromeliads make a cup that holds water. Large plants can hold as much as five litres. Epiphytic orchids have aerial roots hanging down from the branches. Around each root is a layer of non-living, spongy cells called the velamen. When it rains, water soaks into the velamen and is absorbed by the living root.

Aquatic plants

Water plants often have a shortage of oxygen. Plants such as water horsetail (*Equisetum fluviatile*) or water lily (*Nymphaea alba*) have large air spaces in their stems, so that oxygen-containing air can circulate. Mangrove trees live in warm shallow sea water along tropical shores. They root in deep silty mud, where there is little dissolved oxygen. Breathing roots stick out above the surface of the mud. These have many large pores, lenticels, through which air enters.

The fringed water lily (Nymphoides peltata).

Mineral nutrients

The simple sugars made during photosynthesis are the starting point for all the other chemicals that go to make up a plant, but as well as water and sugars, the plant needs mineral nutrients. These are dissolved in soil moisture. Fertile soils contain plenty of different minerals. These leach out from the rocks and clays. A fertile soil also has plenty of organic material in it. This is called humus. It comes from the decaying bodies of tiny soil creatures and bits of dead plants.

Minerals

Plants need five minerals in quite large amounts:

Nitrogen	needed for proteins, chlorophyll, and genetic material
Phosphorus	needed for proteins, respiration, cell membranes and cell division
Potassium	balances the amount of water in the cells
Calcium	needed for cell walls and membranes
Magnesium	needed for chlorophyll
Sulphur	needed for proteins.

In addition, a plant need minute traces of some other chemicals, such as iron, copper and zinc.

Carnivorous plants

There is little dissolved oxygen in the muds of bogs and swamps. This means that decaying organisms cannot thrive, so that a thick layer of dead plants builds up. Nutrients, especially nitrogen, remain locked up inside these remains, so the mud is infertile. Carnivorous plants get an extra supply of nitrogen and other nutrients by trapping insects. They can survive without these nutrients, but will not make as many flowers and seeds.

Leafy traps

Venus fly trap (*Dionaea muscipula*) has spine-edged traps at the tip of each leaf. When a fly lands on these, it triggers a mechanism that closes the trap, to stop the insect escaping, in less than a second.

▶ *This common sundew* (Drosera rotundifolia) *has just caught a lacewing. Sundews have sticky leaves. If small insects land on these, they cannot escape. The leaves curl to enclose the victim and digestive juices ooze out, turning the soft body parts of the insect into liquid full of nutrients. This is absorbed into the leaf.*

Pitcher plants (pictured on the title page) have pitfall traps. The leaves are modified to make water-filled containers with slippery rims. Insects fall in and cannot escape. The largest pitcher plant, *Nepenthes rajah*, from South-east Asia, holds about three litres of water. Small frogs and mice are part of this plant's diet.

Root nodules

Nitrogen gas makes up 78 per cent of the atmosphere. Plants cannot use this nutrient in its gaseous state. Small nodules on the root of plants in the pea family contain nitrogen-fixing bacteria. These change nitrogen gas into substances that the plant can use.

Parasites

A parasitic plant takes all its food and water from another plant. It attaches itself to the roots or stems, and draws water, food and minerals from its host. The host plant is seldom killed – this would also mean that the parasite dies too – but it may not be as healthy.

▲ *Broomrape* (Orobranche elatior) *is a parasitic plant that has lost both leaves and chlorophyll. The tall flower spike makes seeds that cannot grow unless they land close to its host.*

Reproductive success

THE SURVIVAL OF A SPECIES depends on its ability to reproduce itself. Many plants can reproduce sexually and asexually. Sexual reproduction is by means of seeds or spores. Cross-pollination ensures a good mixture of genetic material, but many plants will self-pollinate if all else fails. Asexual, or vegetative reproduction, involves the development of new plants by runners, stolons or bulbils. These offspring are genetically identical to the parent plant.

◀ *Strawberries make new plants by means of runners.*

▼ *Birds, such as this violet sabrewing hummingbird, generally have a poor sense of smell. They are attracted to red or purple flowers with plentiful nectar.*

Pollination

Seed-producing plants need help to transfer the male pollen to the female parts of a flower, or female cone. Wind is one way of achieving this, but it is a matter of chance whether the right pollen lands on its target. Wind-pollinated plants maximise these chances by producing vast quantities of dry, dusty pollen: to see this, try tapping a cluster of ripe hazel catkins.

Insect-pollinated flowers often have pale petals with a sweet scent and droplets of sugary nectar. Flowers that have bats as pollinators tend to have a rancid, cheesy smell and thick, sticky nectar.

Dispersal

If all seeds simply fell from the parent plant, most of them would die in the competition for light and water. Dispersal ensures that seeds are spread out so that more have a chance of surviving. Wind, animals or water all help dispersal. The fruit wall often plays an important part in spreading the seeds of flowering plants.

Seeds of poplar and willowherbs are small, with tufts of cottony hairs to help keep them airborne. The winged seeds of pine help them to drift a good distance from the parent tree, and ash trees have winged fruits that help in the same way.

Plants attract animals to spread their seeds with sweet, juicy fruit. Birds and mammals eat the fruit and either spit out or swallow the seeds. Swallowed seeds eventually pass out in the droppings. Their tough coat prevents them being digested, but the action of the digestive juices softens it so that they germinate more readily.

Other specialists

Some plants have fruits that cling on to fur or feet. The grapple plant fruit is a fearsome hooked capsule that sticks into the feet of elephants or rhinoceroses. It is carried around until the hooked arms break off.

Fruits that rupture explosively shoot their seeds in all directions. These mechanisms are largely powered by parts of the fruit wall drying faster than others. This sets up tensions, causing the fruits to split open. Gorse pods split and twist, flicking out seeds. Just one touch triggers the capsules of Himalayan balsam to rupture.

The thick fibrous husk of a coconut (Cocos nucifera) is coated with a waxy waterproof layer. Air trapped in the husk keeps the coconut afloat as it drifts across the sea, eventually to be washed ashore, where it may germinate.

The future for plants

THIS BOOK GIVES YOU SOME IDEA of the amazing diversity of the plant kingdom. Most of us see many green plants every day, as even in cities there are open spaces and street trees. Rural areas are full of plants, and in just an ordinary garden, a jungle of weeds appears after only a few weeks of neglect. It is hard to realise that many species of plants are on the brink of extinction, and the loss of habitats is making many more species far less abundant than they once were.

Even if you never want to visit a tropical rain forest, you need the services it provides. These huge stretches of forest stabilise the climate. Cutting them down is not only a great loss of natural diversity, but contributes to global warming and causes local soil erosion.

Endangered species

An endangered species is one that is in imminent danger of becoming extinct. There are over 6,000 species of plants that are officially listed as endangered, and about another 400 that may be endangered or already extinct. Over-collection by florists and plant collectors has meant that many have been brought to the verge of extinction.

Tropical forests are rich in plant species. Here, a tree fern is just one many plants in an area of natural rain forest on the island of St Lucia, in the Caribbean.

Botanical gardens

Botanical gardens provide opportunities for recreation and are of great interest to anyone who enjoys plants. These gardens also have a valuable role in plant conservation. They act as reservoirs for plants and their seeds that may become threatened or even extinct in the wild.

The toromiro tree was once abundant on Easter Island but it has been extinct in the wild since 1962. Since then, only a few specimens survived in botanical gardens around the world, but a breeding programme is likely to result in its re-introduction on Easter Island.

Selective breeding

The very first farmers started selective breeding of crop plants by instinctively saving seed from the best plants: the sweetest apples or the fattest ear of wheat. The basics of genetics was not properly understood until the beginning of the twentieth century, when the observations of the Austrian monk Gregor Mendel were discovered. Since then, most crops in cultivation have been improved to give higher yield and better resistance to pests and diseases.

Genetically modified crops

Genetic modification of crops is when a tiny fraction of the genetic material from a quite unrelated organism is put into the genetic material of a crop plant. This gives the modified crop a characteristic that it would otherwise not have, for instance, a high resistance to herbicides. Some genetically modified crops, such as soybeans and tomatoes, are already being grown. While some people believe genetic modification will be the revolutionary science of the twenty-first century, others are worried that these new crops will harm their health. Environmentalists are concerned about the effects on wildlife.

Valuable diversity

As scientists find out more about plants, we realise that even those that we thought were of no use to us are in fact valuable. If we allow plant diversity to dwindle, we may lose these useful but yet undiscovered products. As well as using plants themselves, we also need their woodland, forest, wetland and flowery meadow habitats. We have a duty to conserve all natural resources for future generations.

The aim of genetically modifying plants is to give them different characteristics. Scientists are trying to produce disease-resistant potatoes, so farmers can grow better crops using less pesticide.

Glossary

Aerial roots Roots that grow in the air, and are not covered by soil or water.

Archegonia (sing. archegonium) The male sex organs of liverworts, mosses and ferns.

Botanists People who study plants.

Capsule The spore-bearing structure of a moss or liverwort; also in flowering plants, a kind of dry fruit that opens along particular lines, or pores.

Cell membrane The extremely thin layer that surrounds each cell.

Chlorophyll A green pigment that traps the energy in sunlight for photosynthesis.

Cross-pollinate When pollen from the flowers of one plant pollinate the flowers of another plant of the same species.

Dormant An inactive, or resting stage in seeds and buds which prevents them from germinating or opening in unfavourable weather conditions.

Embryo The very young stage of a plant that develops after the female sex cell has been fertilised by a male sex cell.

Evaporation Loss of water vapour into the air.

Evolve To develop naturally over a long period of time, usually but not always by means of very small changes.

Fertile A soil that is rich in plant nutrients and moisture; seed- or spore-bearing parts of a plant; and a seed or spore that is capable of growing into a new plant.

Flagella (sing. flagellum) A microscopically small hair-like structure that lashes to cause movement.

Gametophyte The haploid stage in the life cycle of plants during which the sex cells are produced.

Germinate When a seed or spore starts to grow.

Habitats The places in which plants, animals or a community of plants and animals, live.

Herbaceous A plant with non-woody stems.

Infertile A soil that is poor in plant nutrients; or a seed or spore that is not capable of growth no matter how favourable the conditions.

Leach out When the passage of water removes soluble nutrients and other chemicals from soils.

Mangrove swamps Areas of mangrove trees found in shallow tropical waters at the mouths of river estuaries or along sheltered muddy coasts.

Nectar A sweet liquid produced by many flowers.

Nutrients Essential substances that provide nourishment for the maintenance of life in plants, animals and other living organisms.

Organic material Substances in soil or water that have come from the decayed bodies of living organisms.

Organisms Living things.

Ovule A structure in flowering plants and conifers that develops into a seed after fertilisation.

Palaeontologists People who study fossils.

Peristome teeth Minute teeth around the opening of a moss spore capsule; in dry air, they lose water and twist to help flick out the spores.

Phloem *see* **Vascular tissues**.

Photosynthesis The process in which the energy in sunlight is harnessed by the green pigment (chlorophyll) in plants, to produce sugar from water in the plant and carbon dioxide from the air. Oxygen is also produced as a waste product.

Pigments (+ accessory pigments) Coloured compounds found in plants and other organisms. Accessory pigments trap wavelengths of sunlight that chlorophyll pigments cannot, and transmit the energy gained to the photosynthetic process.

Pollen Minute grains, usually powdery, containing the male sex cells of conifers and flowering plants.

Pollinate To transfer pollen from the male parts of a cone or flower to the female parts of a cone or flower.

Prothallus (pl. prothalli) The usually small, weak gametophyte of a fern, horsetail or clubmoss.

Resins Sticky substances that ooze out of conifer wood or bark when it is damaged.

Respiration Chemical reactions between sugars in a plant's cells and oxygen. They release energy, water and carbon dioxide.

Rhizoids Thread-like structures that help to anchor mosses, liverworts and fern prothalli to the ground or other surface. Some are able to absorb moisture and dissolved minerals.

Sporophyte The diploid stage in the life cycle of plants.

Tectonic plates The rigid sheets of rock that make up the Earth's outer crust.

Temperate woodland Woodland that grows north of the Tropic of Cancer and south of the Tropic of Capricorn.

Tundra The treeless plains of the Arctic and Antarctic regions.

Vascular system The whole arrangement of vascular, or conducting, tissues in a plant.

Vascular tissues Strands of cells (**xylem** and **phloem**) that carry water, dissolved sugars, and other dissolved nutrients around a plant.

Xylem *see* **Vascular tissues**.

Further information

Books

Atlas of Endangered Resources by Steve Pollock (Belitha, 1995)

A Closer Look at Orchids, Palms, Toadstools and Other Green Plants by Jen Green (Watts, 1998)

The Living World: A Visual Factfinder by Brian Williams (Kingfisher, 1997)

The Nature and Science of Leaves by Jane Burton & Kim Taylor (Watts, 1997)

Nature Encyclopedia (Dorling Kindersley, 1998)

Usborne Spotters Guides: Trees & Wild Flowers (Usborne, 1978)

Visual Dictionary of Plants (Dorling Kindersley, 1992)

Magazines

Plant Talk: A quarterly magazine with news and views on plant conservation worldwide
The Botanical Information Company Ltd
P.O.Box 500, Kingston-upon-Thames,
Surrey KT2 5XB

Posters

Classifying Plants (Chart and Notes) by Roger Hore (PCET, 1997)

CD-Roms

Exploring Land Habitats (Wayland, 1997)
Exploring Water Habitats (Wayland, 1997)

Useful addresses and web sites

Fauna and Flora International
Great Eastern House, Tenison Road
Cambridge CB1 2DT

Plantlife: Plant Conservation Charity
21 Elizabeth Street,
London SW1W 9RP

The Natural History Museum
Cromwell Road, London SW7 5BD
www.nhm.ac.uk/education

WWF-UK (World Wide Fund for Nature)
Panda House, Weyside Park
Godalming, Surrey GU7 1XR
www.wwf-uk.org

Photo acknowledgements

Cover: Bruce Coleman: inset/far left (Steve Haufman), inset/centre (Hans Reinhard), inset/far right (Dr Stephen Coyne); Natural History Photographic Agency: main picture (Martin Harvey), inset/second from left (Stephen Kraseman); Tony Stone: inset/second from right (Kerrick James).
Inside: Bruce Coleman: title page (Marie Read), 5 (William S. Paton), 9 (P. Clement), 10 (Jeff Foott Productions), 13 (Hans Reinhard), 16 (John Shaw), 19 (Hans Reinhard), 22 (Allan G. Potts), 30 (Hans Reinhard), 31 (Harald Lange), 33 (Hans Reinhard), 34 (Dr Eckart Pott), 37 (Luiz Claudio Marigo), 38 (John Cancalosi), 41 (left/Kim Taylor), 41 (right/Goerge McCarthy), 42 (bottom/M. P. L. Fogden); Natural History Photo Library: 6 (Laurie Campbell), 11 (Jane Gifford), 12 (N. A. Callow), 18 (Eric Soder), 21 (Stephen Dalton), 25 (Laurie Campbell), 29 (right/Pavel German), 36 (Laurie Campbell), 39 (Hellio and Van Inden), 42 (top/G.I. Bernard); Oxford Scientific Films: 15 (David Fox); 26 (Deni Bown), 29 (left/Michael Leach), 43 (John Brown); Science Photo Library: 45 (Peter Menzel). Tony Stone: 8 (Terry Donnelly), 20 (Joe Cornish), 23 (Jack Dykinga). Wayland Picture Library: imprint page, 27 (Julia Waterlow), 32, 44.
Artwork: page 5 by Simon Borrough: all other artwork by Peter Bull Art Studio.

Index